WHINNY
MOOR
CROSSING

PRINCETON SERIES OF CONTEMPORARY POETS

For Other Books in the Series,
see page 96

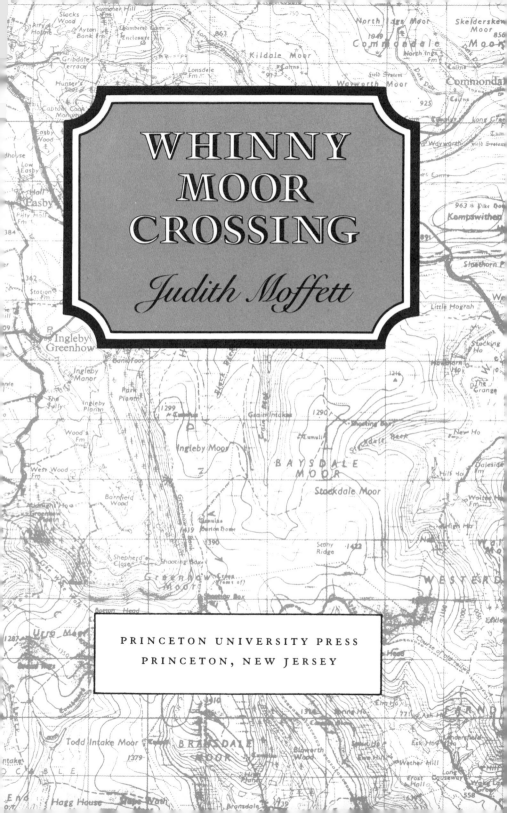

WHINNY MOOR CROSSING

Judith Moffett

PRINCETON UNIVERSITY PRESS

PRINCETON, NEW JERSEY

Library of Congress Cataloging in Publication Data will be
found on the last printed page of this book

ISBN 0-691-06591-8
ISBN 0-691-01410-8 pbk.

Publication of this book has been aided by
a grant from the Paul Mellon Fund
of Princeton University Press

This book has been composed in Linotron Granjon
Clothbound editions of Princeton University Press books
are printed on acid-free paper, and binding materials are
chosen for strength and durability

Printed in the United States of America by
Princeton University Press
Princeton, New Jersey

CREDITS

The poems in this collection first appeared in the following:

Poetry: Passage, Going to Press, Blackout, Relay, Moving Parts,
    Twinings Orange Pekoe, Leaf Lesson
Poetry Miscellany: The Myrtle Warbler
Shenandoah: Gingerbread Ladies, Family Planning, Rainforest
The Little Magazine: Souvenir Sestina, Mezzo Cammin
Quarterly West: After Shelley
The Kenyon Review: Scatsquall in Spring, Reaching Around
Woman Poet/The East: "Cambridge University Swimming Club . . ."
Carolina Quarterly: Whinny Moor Crossing
Iowa Review: Walk with the River
kayak: Found Poems
New England Review: Missing Person
Prairie Schooner: From the Audubon Report (October),
    All Saints Day, The Greenfly Question, Will
Missouri Review: The Old Country, Lucia Day (from
    Advent Calendar 1976)
Laurel Review: The Spellbinding, January Starlings (Curio 1)

ACKNOWLEDGMENTS

A number of these poems were written thanks to the assistance and generosity of the Corporation of Yaddo, the Ingram Merrill Foundation, and the University of Pennsylvania's Faculty Research Grants program. I am very grateful to each of these institutions for its support.

The prose quotations in " 'Cambridge University Swimming Club / No Public Access to River' " are taken from *Period Piece: A Cambridge Childhood*, by Gwen Raverat, first published in 1952 by Faber & Faber Limited.

The five "Found Poems" were discovered in Chapter 10, "Female Song, Duetting, and Corporate Song" (pp. 178-79), of *A Study of Bird Song*, by Edward A. Armstrong, published in London by the Oxford University Press in 1963.

CONTENTS

WHINNY
MOOR
CROSSING

PASSAGE

The book's done. Half-packed cartons
hunch gaping on the carpet; their wide flaps
tremble or wave as lifting bare legs
I stalk and stalk among them, distractedly
stooping, poking, cramming. That late April
I lighted here, plucked breast-down
and lined this hollow and settled in,
it was in hopes of never again ... but lately
since the fat fledgling brain child left
the place feels used up. I wholly see
why mother storks, knowing a nest was ever
only a cradle, clack to each other: Let's leave
all this now to its lice and whitewash. High
time again! Come, shove off, let's get moving.

For all that being footloose is pure American,
is being homeless, really? Even our Don't-Fence-Me-In
frontier colossi—trapper, riverman, cowpoke, buffalo-
hunter, halfbreed scout—all seem unspeakably
at home in dangerous and absorbing lives
whose skills, weapons, rituals had to be
portable as a Cheyenne tipi (the Plains nomads
were rooted in one another, as in the wide grasslands
they crossed and recrossed, following the migrant herds,
unimaginably). A pioneer was only a seedling
settler. Someplace else his life had chafed him;
now he prodded his oxen west, skinny wife
jouncing on the seat, kids and plow in the cartbed,
looking out sharp for likely land.

3

It was bound to start rootless; the immense continent
made enduring a life that chafed downright foolish
if one were hardy and young. But homeless?
There was once a frontier settlement called
Boonesborough. Its founder, "a legend in his own lifetime,"
strayed west in stiff, furious, real old age.
The game was gone, the place felt used up,
the frontier had melted clean off to Colorado.
And that virgin Kentucky wilderness he'd been
first of his race to penetrate, delighted in,
lain on his back and sung to, was ruined.
He could blame himself. Daniel Boone died homeless,
homesick for a lost state. But rootless?

Films are dubbed or inaudible, important books
translated, and English universal;
yet every day in Stockholm, where I'm writing this,
a few more inessential Swedish words
get worried into my brain. Why bother?
From horticultural instinct, apparently,
grasping how all the long roots I have
are snarled for dear life in a language.

The young cactus slip I set in water
sent forth white filaments in search of something
to take hold of; it's nature. Later, when these were threads,
I patted loose earth about them. Since then
I've let them be. More and more I feel
how they'd sooner snap than turn loose now.

We'll come back next spring, the storks
assure each other, make new nests with new sticks
on top of these, and white eggs and chicks,
and the next spring and the next.

A doubtful metaphor, by the way: America
never had storks, nor do they any longer
return to breed in Sweden. Do the storks
know anything I don't?

I think often of emigrating to England.
There's precedent, why not? Marry
a don or a BBC actor, stay warm on the world's best
tea, stay true to Form as to Wimsey? Stay?

Ghost oxcart jolting east, tall-rigged ghost ship *Pioneer*
homing on Bristol harbour . . .

I wrote on Exmoor looking north to where
The footpath scrambled down through sheep and heather
Toward Wooton Courtenay. Drought had kept the
    weather
Perfect, though strangely brownish; loud blue air

Stroked the moor's thrilling contours like a hand.
Backpack and boots behind me in the flowers
How fine! How wild somehow to tramp for hours
In high long view of cultivated land!

"10 miles today over the open moor. I'm sitting on a
breezy slope so thick with heather and fern
(bracken?) the whole hill must look purple-and-green from
    that town
down there. Slight haze but a perfectly cloudless day,

and"—out of nowhere—"*what am I doing here?*"

Automatic writing. The last loose year.

ONE
Stockholm

FOR
HENRIETTA BOTHÉN
AND TO THE MEMORY OF
DR. NILS FREDRIK LEONARD BOTHÉN

GOING TO PRESS

Those close Denver evenings I'd drag myself
down to the green though treeless "park"
hemmed by light traffic, construction sites, a hospital,
whose reedy seepage deepened, widened, doing
all it could to assert pondhood. Sprinklers
would be hurling ack-ack. Down I'd flop
into that start of coolness, watch little fish
dimple the surface, lip flies and flip out
flightily, plop-plop-plop like a skipped stone.
They soothed me, some. I'd think about the moors.

An hour's drive and a full day's exhaust fumes
stretched out between park and pond and the Front Range now
further smudged by dusk, posing a low profile
cut out of soft black construction paper
with kindergarten scissors, a set
for the melodrama Sunset. Wrenchingly desirable.
Impossibly remote. Flung there instead
I'd feel my unplugged brain click
like an iron cooling, its root system of fine
wires threaded through abdomen and back
lose pitch: tic tic (space) tic.

Those hag-ridden evenings I fathomed this—
some in extremis can look for no relief
save through increase only. *Press* the Swedes say
naming the state of strain, that desperate state,
and humble me again
to hear Giles Corey, aged family man
killed for a witch in Salem, flat on his back
in a green field the final days of his dying,
crushingly burdened, breathless, swollen, protruding,
croak his two words: More weight.

9

Blackout

The old people of Gärdet (my part of Stockholm) are
oddly many and visible. Every day
one sees them cautiously groping at the patterned
paving stone with two canes. Nearly all
are women in long dark coats and hats
decently pinned straight. Between brim and collar
faces like china light can pass through
look hesitant, preoccupied. The old ladies
already know that each time they venture forth
to shop for bread and coffee, blond schoolkids
are going to crash into them—girls
clattering like ponies on their wooden soles
in shrill pursuit of boys who in fifty years,
still ahead, will have begun to die.
The kids bounce off, careen away blindly;
the infirm old widows totter. You can tell
how they dread speed, abruptness, heavy doors,
falling worst of all; but there's nobody to send.

2

Every day, out for my five-mile loop by the water,
I see them poking along, preoccupiedly
putting each cane's rubber toecot down
upon stone. The air is dull autumn's;
too late—again—already!—to rest on a safe
sunsoaked park bench while naked babies
splash in the fountain pools. Each buys what she needs
and makes her way home, shivering. Every day
in jeans and jacket and joggers I flash past them.
I'm half their age—less—I can trot a mile
in nine minutes. Right now, this instant,

soft cloth clasping my calf and thigh muscles
kindly, shoes mounted on springs, blood
fizzing like hard cider, I'm already half as old
as many of them; and of late I feel my three dozen
gray hairs tense in their follicles,
pierce the scalp, and my hip joints
remember their brief creakiness at waking,
whenever Gärdet's army of black widows passes
by ones and twos haltingly in review.

3

Black-and-white silent movie: the set
a pale sky, soft and low above white spurting
fountains; a path that follows a canal
darkly flowing seaward, the mezzo cammin. Action:
my tireless self in its gray sweat suit
jogs up the path, nimbly dodging
sticklike figures propped on sticks
in long coats, barely moving but so many.
Moving my way. Soundlessly, breathing easily,
I lope round each from behind, but black canes
and the back of black coats
keep creeping on, up ahead, sparse yet far
as I can see. Gradually I perceive
with a heavy settling certainty
they can't all be outdistanced, and I turn
jogging in place to face them. And see
what I never saw till now: how their trappings,
fears, frailties, the close companion death—
all they have in common—might count
for less than all
that witnesses in those porcelain faces, saying
Spite   Pluck   Serenity   Wonder
saying   *My life was a trap   Mine was a stair*
A beach   A moonscape   Silent

they cripple forward, bright and dark
in separate eloquence.
Their old eyes, preoccupied, look
elsewhere, they do not know themselves
what the odds are. Jogger wheels round,
picks up the pace, the scene goes gray. Fadeout.

FROM THE AUDUBON REPORT (OCTOBER)

... by day, disturbing
scatter-rugs of Sparrows patter
and feed among the dead
leaves like leaves,
backs brown and blade-shaped, then
like blown leaves whirl
away together. (Naturally
they'll winter over.) And at first and last light
a vast pillow-fight of silhouettes
clutters the sky, alighting
and lurching free—
the tall rooftops, the beaten air between
shrieking in agitation: *tchack! tchack!* A park's
double row of moulting
horse chestnuts vacuums them up
as full dark falls. They roost restless,
pestered by magpies, excited by passing headlights,
crying out together all hours of the night.
These are the birds called *kajor*
(KI yoor)—Jackdaws, Crows
of a sort; by day
seen scrappily charging Pigeons or
marching, singly, large
and sinister, planting firmly their
six hard clawgrip toes ...

13

RELAY

October: daylight narrowing like an eye.
Now for the sunless season—long nights, gray
days of permanent twilight. But for now
big yellow leaves glow down
still parted and pushed like hair upon
black branches that release them
continually, glow up from the ground
they cover, making
a yellow place to pause in, invoking
sun where no sun is, beside the waterways.
To ease us in. High seasonal winds
risen like the tide crinkle
this inlet's foil surface west, against
its slow prevailing
current, away from the open sea.

Coot,
hadn't you better come ashore?
How can he stand it? His poor toes—
their oak-leaf scallops must be numb!
How can he just go on
clutching his way by the usual rapid
footfuls through this choppy
ice-pale lakewater?
At least today he isn't diving. Other coots
paddle past; but the subdued
mallards, bills clenched to breasts, float
immobilized behind backwater-
windbreaks of tufted reeds
like Moses in his basket; at the thought of
the little orange leaf-shapes dangling
under them in the murk,
my eyebrows ache.

Lobed oak, triple-toebone webbed maple ...
tons of bushels of leaves the wind
dumps here along the long
canal bank, to be sunk deep or worked
into the floating faded mats of linden
leaves. One day soon, if they happen to look up,
these huddled ducks
will see through stripped black branches
as if through lashes
how the tall trees have lapsed,
exposing each
its crow or two, or cold squirrel's nest
snarled in the crown;
will waddle past those drowned
footprints, pressing leafprints in snow:
webbed, with three branching veins.
Soon. And on that day
an owl's amber eye, if you can ever
catch it, will show you the only yellow
light left in this world. Sun
into leaf; sun to moon to owl-
glare. November's heavy lid, lowering.

Moving Parts

Stress concentrates in joints, just
where the joined parts hold or flex together.
After a shift of use and wear
the grease rubs patchy, the ligature
stretches, loosens, frays. Think of linked
boxcars; think what lost pitch is
and tennis elbow. Loves are like that,
surviving if lubed/tuned up to their own
frequency, and if not, not. What
do people expect? They will go on
changing, and then Connection's willful too.
A cat whose humans keep forgetting
his dinner, who leave him out in the rain,
moves on. By the time they've missed him
he's miles away, he won't be caught again.

The whole history of couplings
teaches how crazy it is to just let
moving parts look after
themselves, assume they'll always
fit snug and turn smoothly. Instead
they ache or fuse or separate. It seems
Connection's an austere, a temperamental,
a damageable marvel
we're meant to prove we've earned, and that
everyday benign existing
proves nothing of the sort. Best face it: on a world
where particles dance in solution
where continents drift
the oldest and truest of your friends
could, without warning
and for no reason he knows,
wake one morning having ceased
to wish you well. He could. He probably will.

For nothing's fixed or finished,
not till we're dead. Yet *nothing* is; I know
we are not doomed
only to disconnection. No unrequited
lover can ever swear
time's chances and changes and his own fine-tuned
care for those again, or still,
remote in indifference or fear
won't finally gentle them,
or some of them, or one. Eight Octobers back
in this same small cold country,
how could my wildest fantasy have dared
far-fetch the two of us
onto a Front Range boulder, happy and calm,
bell-clear Elk Creek talking, sun-colored aspens
swarming the mountainside? But we
were there; and now we're here, and now
something let in each evening
pads into the firelight to lap
on the hearth warmed for its coming
a gleaming saucer clean, and furl to sleep.

ALL SAINTS DAY

Skillfully the crisscross of bare twigs
above this sloping well-kept churchyard
snares the first moon to slip cloud cover
in a month—a full moon, having
waned and waxed unseen, and risen tonight
robust again as ever. By light that rare
through November dusk we've come
to the chill heart of Stockholm,
behind the Nordic Museum, to observe a custom
borrowed from Germany after the war.

Dutiful kin have been out in force before us.
Most of these tidy military graves now lie
tucked under coverlets of pine, the same dark
boughs, and wreaths wired shut
with ribbons and cones, whose green-black heaps outside
every flower shop and food store in town
have been baffling me all week. Now
I see they weren't for Christmas, weren't
even for doors. ("The portal—in the ground"—
almost a Dickinson variant—won't come to mind
for days, yet at once I recognize the way
a small tin on either side of each headstone
holds its clear pool of waxmelt
thick stiff morel-shaped wick
and yellow flame: it's just the way
a festive Swedish doorway tells arriving guests
where the party is.)
                    Sharp still evening,
windless, candle-scented. Hennie and Freddie
search for ten minutes with a pocket flashlight
for Freddie's Tant Greta's grave, then feel sad
that she has no lights or greenery. Well,

this year this cemetery has none for sale.
Nothing to be done. We mount the path of sand
for a moonlit view of the city
water-skirted and bridge-buckled, black silk lakes
outspread, enfolding us. When we turn back
                                        the graveyard
is a Disney memory of figure-skating
fairies come out spontaneous as stars,
will-o'-the-wisps self-kindled to Tchaikovsky
in frost and darkness; and is
the Scandinavian essence that most takes
substance near the morning of deepest dark,
the coldest morning, in Lucia's crown of candles—
or crown of light; for *light* and *candles* share
a single Swedish word. Made not flesh but flame.

Across and down the slope
a thousand yellow eyes flicker, tricking
ours while we stare, making them water and keep
needing to blink, blink, shrink and sharpen
all those blurrily expanding foxfire globes
to the slips of flame they are. Gently they illumine
a verticality of treetrunks and gray
gravestones, plain slow downstrokes repeated,
blending out of blackness into
firelight, stopping cold
at the ground. You'd have to paint it, though,
this scene, if you did, with upward
brushstrokes, technique not fact preserving
the downwardness we see. It's what
we do see. For all they make the eye
drop, these stones stand utterly still.
Their yellow flames pulse sideways. We start downhill.

Twinings Orange Pekoe

The gas ring's hoarse exhaling wheeze,
Voice of blue flamelets, licks the kettle's
Copper underbelly, which crouches
Closer, concentrates, by degrees

Begins spellbound to match that pressure
And dragon tone. Breath crowds the slim
Tranced throat that cannot close or scream;
It spouts a rushing *whooo* of pleasure.

The brown potbellied pot, top doffed,
Reveals its scalded insides' tender
Nursery blue, from which a cloud
Exudes, and from its spout a slender

Curl. It sweats and loves the *tch*
A lid makes popping off a tin,
The fragrance deep as leafmold, rich
As pipe tobacco, coffee, cocoa;

Loves the spoon's dry *scroop*, the skin-
Tight leafheap scattered in its breast
(A tannic prickle); the swift boiling
Flashflood, spoonswirl, settling flight; loves best

The steeping in the dark: blind alchemy:
Tap water, and an acid that cures leather
Stains cups and eats through glazes, pregnantly
Stewing together,

To arch forth in a stream as brown and bright
And smoky as an eye, strain marbling up
Through milk and sugar in a stoneware cup,
White white on white.

GINGERBREAD LADIES

Through slush and lightly pelting
BB pellets of snow to the public
bastu (the Finnish word *sauna*
steams, and the sign says DAMTURK)

the big old one at Stureplan. Leaving
all your clothes in your curtained-off
cubbyhole you descend a staircase,
receive your towel sponge soapcake

from a gargoyle gowned in white,
enter a door and take your place upon
a deck chair's wooden slats among still
female forms disposed like so much

pastry dough swelling in a hot hot
oven—copper ceiling, three walls
and floor of tile. The corridor wall
is glass; we might be waxworks in some

museum exhibit of Scandinavian custom.
You settle down for the twenty
or so minutes it will take your skin
to achieve the proper wet flushed

blotchiness; chat; snooze, some, having
good eyes or contact lenses, pass this
time with paperbacks they don't mind giving
a rained-on warp to. At the right moment,

then, a hard shower and two eye-popping
laps of the tiny icy pool that does
instead of snow. Repeat: short
sweat shower plunge. After a final

and more elaborate shower the kindly
gargoyle helps you into a white robe
inwoven STUREBADET. (Someplace
in the HERRTURK at this point

Freddie's submitting to the massage
I'm too cheap to pay for.) Finally
half an hour prone and tingling on
the cot in your own cubicle under a light

blanket, where you can order a coffee
and *smörgås* like any blood donor
before plunging again into clothes
and overcoat and snowstorm street

where still will be stepping the tall
thoroughbred that plopped his aloof
huge hoof in slush, shooting a gray blob
splat at my throat, on our way here.

SMOKE

C.H.D., 1909-1977

On doctor's orders you spent whole days
in bed, your cough so tearing
it wore you out. Double pneumonia.
All that dark fall
I brought the sickroom bright
seasonal trinkets, red
leaves or horse chestnuts I now see
must have struck you
as maddeningly beside the point.
One raw afternoon your raccoon coat
charged toward me in the street,
hesitated, pushed on defiant.
Out? In this weather? Guiltily
you pleaded stir-craziness, but at once I knew
now smoke would seep again
under the bathroom door.

Should I have tried to stop you
then and there? Beautiful, gaunt, smudge-eyed
brittle tree of a woman,
as weak as furtive, might you have let me? I
whom you permitted
to nurse and shop, do laundry, make
beds and soups, who would have moved
mountains to have you well
or fallen trying, could not be asked to help you kill
yourself; but to stay by and keep still
rather than shame you, *that*
was possible—not that you thought it through!
Simply, a live-in jailer suited you,
and I

23

proved manageable. Not love but trust went up
in smoke forever.
Simply, we lived your lie.

Knowing your own ways, you chose this.
All the next autumn
passed in a hospital bed.
Cancer. Lung, then bone and brain;
white-gray waves a rolling
blur on the pillow, long shanks
ridging the blanket. No more jailbreaks
from pain, or nightmares—
enemies, terrors—or the good intentions
of friends. How
many dozens of us
had literally adored you? To this day
I hate it that you loved and needed anything
more than your crowded life,
and family in Monza, and me. Tonight
safe at home by a fireside
you'll never share,
from cold that won't again
smoke with your breath, I miss you
and am still angry.

10 *A large letter N on a television screen*

Having been twice already (Kawabata, White)
let into the Awards Ceremony—admired
the brass trumpets, stood while the Royal
Family, glittering, very far below, filed in
once led by the good old King, once
by the brand-new blond one, seen great
men in the (distant) flesh, and much enjoyed
the pomp and fuss that understandably
mark the single day each year when the world's
attention briefly turns this way—this time
I've taken the ticket shortage gracefully
and settled for live TV. Millions like me
are watching as the audience turns and cranes now,
trying to figure out the sudden commotion
somewhere in its privileged midst; at home,
at work, out shopping, the rest of us lean
toward our sports fan's zoom-shot closeup of . . .
an agitator of some sort? . . . yes, cleverly
disguised in a tuxedo, interrupting a speech
to carry on, and on, about Milton Friedman,
the Laureate in Economics (standing now, ready
to come and take his Prize "from the hands
of His Majesty the King") who's lectured
in many countries, including Eastern Europe's,
and also once in Chile. *Frihet till Chile!*
squeaks the agitator, waving his arms,
while four policemen gingerly extract him,
toothlike, from a seat in the packed
Concert House so much better than mine
ever was, or would or will be, that by
foreign scholars perched up near the ceiling
the invisible disturbance they hardly hear
goes, they'll say later, almost unremarked.

Nobody here could feel surprised, exactly;
the Radical Left, desperate for something
to stand and act against, these days, has been
nothing if not outspoken against Friedman,
over this Chile business, from the hour
the Bank of Stockholm announced its choice.
Still, the world's looking on. *"Skandal!"*
Hennie, who works for the Moderates, will shortly
fume on the phone. There's one here somewhere.
At least, the next day's scandal sheets
will live well up to type, each excitedly
blazoning its interview with the youthful
creep they're calling "the tux man"
in tall black banners that explain the motive:
"I wished to demonstrate my loathing."

(Imagine somebody, a priest, a teacher, coming
downstage instead, polite though unexpected,
to tell us Friedman is the gentlest of men,
so kind to animals and old folks, so
patient, so generous, such a splendid
moral example to young economists, "Forgive me,
I wished to demonstrate my love"—
would Cronkite or *Expressen* care? Ho hum,
no conflict. Yet, shades of the late sixties, *now*
three network newscasters at home are fated
to speak tonight of this, and PBS's
viewers to think about it soon: the crew
sent to film the all-American event
filmed the tux man and his loathing too—
his, but by nature promptly self-inflated.)

On the screen now, apologies are tendered
inaudibly to Friedman in the young King's,
Carl Gustav's, English; Friedman hangs onto
his tense grin and gets the day's biggest hand.

He's bigger *news* for being loathed.
Media will make him, more than ever,
their creature now, begin in fact to sway
the public to a friendlier backlash. Three
mornings more and our sober daily
will unfold itself upon a page one photo:
Friedman—none of the others, Bellow
for example (who here could loathe Bellow?)—
smiling in pajamas, caught by the flash
just opening his Grand Hotel room door upon
Lucia: serenade, crown, tray of good things.

12 *A heart-shaped book*

Freddie tells anecdotes about the aged
Academicians now slowly filling their VIP
section (we're at Saul Bellow's Nobel Lecture):
how, years back, one old gentleman published
a book of "absurd" "poems" jerry-built
by himself and a friend, two brash young doctors,
in a single hilarious night over some *smörgåsar*
and beers for a gag—he reading out
dictionary words at random, his friend
writing them down—except that reviewers
raved and the book, *Camera obscura*, was bringing
$65 in '73—not that Freddie would give
ten times that for *his* copy! And how
another, bent and stout now, had long ago
been Hennie's dinner partner at a society
wedding, and sent her roses afterwards (and will,
in 48 hours, in Geneva, drop dead—a heart attack
no part of Freddie's story, only of mine).

Bellow, dark suit and cropped white head, comes on
to deprecate, after some stirring words about
Conrad and character, a separation
in the West between writers of genius

and the general public, deplore
a contempt for the "average reader" who,
he asserts with obvious conviction,
immensely desires that literature return
to the center of the "main human enterprise"
and be simple and true.
                              Simple *and* true? ...
the mind balks, I stop following. For if truths
are simple expressed in trim formulae
—$E = mc^2$, "the greatest of these is charity"—
still, in human affairs, where's
principle? Applied like sludge to lives
in situations appallingly complex, where Meaning
kicks and squalls, that's where. Isn't Hiroshima
the whole truth for an average reader? Never
the cold pure numbers in whose beauty alone
a Werner von Braun can be comprehended,
and in whose simple answers (wrote Bronowski
speaking of Einstein's work) "we hear God
thinking." SB's own blip—just listen to him!—
lights up pretty far off-center; he's known all this
longer and better than I have. What's going on?

Freddie has so-so English and must concentrate,
frowning hard. I keep having trouble too.
The language is abstract, and I'm distracted,
straining to picture a public that mostly reads,
when it does, the mouldering-ruined romantic
and the fanged horrific in paperback originals
plus serenity/ecstasy/orgasm nonfiction, folding
a present-day Tolstoy or Dickens to its breast;
am fumbling to grasp within the cloud of words
their speaker's purpose in professing
before the world, from the limelit lectern
his for this Sabbath day, the faith that literature
might pound once more at its heart.

28

A press-conference stratagem, maybe:
to state as truth *accompli* something
you mean, or hope, to conjure true if only
you're believed. Maybe simply plumping
for truths to be fleshed out again in fiction
is purpose enough. Maybe it's not even
simplistic or simple-minded or a lie
to imply that'd change anything. And maybe too
I'm missing some of what he means. Still
across the floor of these thoughts
a draft keeps blowing—
of a Herzog letter, maybe. Maybe just wind.

13 *A yellow candleflame on black*

Shadows of fat snowflakes whirl on snow
hugely under the streetlamps; I'm
struggling up a drifted hill
otherwise black as timeless at 6 a.m.
Five floors high, Hennie releases the downstairs door
with a magic button. Silver and porcelain
shine round her centerpiece of four
thick white candles at a green wreath's cardinal
points. More candles dartle everywhere,
and tabletops, eyes, dozens of gleaming bibelots,
polished coffee- and teapots, plates piled with the saffron
whorls called *lussekatter*, with sliced *stollen*
(Dutch Hennie was a girl in München)
catch, hold, flash back candleflame
highlights as in a still life by Vermeer.
Dazzled, I stand my boots to melt in the hall.

6:30. Freddie wakes the TV set
across whose screen unsteady lights become
candles borne by a file of white-haired white-
robed children from a rural church-school choir.
They wind toward the beautiful country home

of the late painter Carl Larsson, in Dalarna in the dark
North, singing in unison, like flutes,
something familiar—a standard gondolier
number, but with the fulsome Mediterranean
in wholly Baltic straits.
The boys with Starboy trappings—tall
duncecaps, star-tipped Blue Fairy wands—are mere
attendant lords for once; the girls go bareheaded, all
but lucky Lucia, soloist in her prickly crown.
She steps, the little flames bend back,
elongate, smoke. She represents an eldest daughter
making the rounds of bedrooms long before daybreak,
bearing her serving tray of cups and plates,
coffee and *lussekatter*,
singing the song. Her voice is true and clear.

> *Night stalks with heavy tread*
> *Barnyards and meadows,*
> *Round earth where sun has fled*
> *Brood the deep shadows.*
> *Then through our darkened homes,*
> *Tall candles lighted, comes*
> *Sankta Lu-see-a,*
> *Sankta Lucia.*

Freddie remarks that formerly Lucias
used to burn like Christmas trees; their hair'd
catch fire . . . nowadays the crowns come battery-powered.
We feast by candlelight while the snow flies.

It wouldn't be light for hours, snow or no snow.

Inside, the choir switches to carols now.
When the show's over, I'll plow home in the dark.
Later, crossing the park
after a nap and a stretch of work,
I'll spot a girl of ten or so stomping along,

the thin white gown she's wearing under her coat
over her woollen snowpants bunching and clinging,
crown in a paper bag. Four years ago
this Volvo-headlit afternoon, caught
in the subway's Central Station with a rowdy throng
of Starboys and Lucias coming back
from school Lucia parties, Hennie heard
that welter of kids be stirred
spontaneously into their corny song
as by a wind across a cornfield, singing
louder and louder, at last the whole horde.
Today, she tells me, most schools will stay shut;
so many twelve-year-olds were getting so
drunk at those parties; but how I love
to imagine that wide echoing steel-gray cave
startling unSwedishly to the timbre of
hundreds of trebles, words too sweet to believe:

> *Darkness from dale and hill*
> *Soon shall be driven,*
> *So she a wonderful*
> *Promise has given.*
> *Soon, day anew shall rise*
> *Fair through the rosy skies.*
> *Sankta Lucia,*
> *Sankta Lucia.*

TWO
Cambridge

FOR
THE CLUB REGULARS

SOUVENIR SESTINA

Darting, leaning, fleetly the blue bicycle
Rings at blind corners, parts the puddles of rain
In two smooth swatches, climbs over the river
By a humped bridge and swishes down like wildfire
Through shoppers, bikes, cars, trucks of dirt, of milk,
Toward home—or toward the place it lives, a house.

There's the green gate. The rider rounds the house,
Puffing, to stash away the trusty bicycle.
A paper depresses the letterslot's tongue. Milk
Waits on the stoop, still cold. The chill spring rain
Breeds damp; inside she switches on the fire.
One bar glows red. And soon, the way a river

Slides over flat rocks, rain streams in a river
Over the panes again. Life in this house
Means inconvenience, an electric fire
Being neither hearth nor furnace and a bicycle
Awkward in such a season of daily rain,
Though splendid in its way. But astonishing milk

In glass bottles, with hats of yellow topmilk,
Comes daily too and every day the river
Is there to walk or bike by; and now, while rain
Lashes the windows of the stucco house,
The kettle's boiled, both she and the swift bicycle
Are tucked up snug. She draws a chair to the fire,

Brings to a table set by chair and fire
Scones: teacup: teapot: jampot: jug of milk:
The Masters (Snow). It's hungry work to bicycle
Fast into town tossed on a fuming river
Of traffic, rush through errands and back to the house,
Flying before low windclouds black with rain!

The house of memory will be sheathed in rain
But bright within, and cozy. By the fire
Tea will be laid. Clinking up to the house
A milkman with his wire caddy of milk.
And locked to a pasture fencepost where the river
Bends with its ducks and punts, a rust-flecked bicycle.

Later, if the rain clears off, she'll bicycle
To watch the river flow with honey and milk,
And over the house the washed-out clouds catch fire.

After Shelley

The Anxiety of Influence

By following up
the sound—flute with a Highland burr—
to its source, you'll spot him
larking, fly-tiny, wings awhirr,
or else afloat on open
wings, high or very high
over flat fen pastureland. Climbing
he flickers in the eyes
the way no flicker does, that flies
exactly like a scissors; hung
lower against the sun, light filters through
the tense extended tips of all
his flight feathers wing and tail; and then
a brightness borders him.

The famous song begins
when he's fluttered up and clear of the place
under the grass where his nest
hides, or will shortly hide, in a hoofprint
to spill down, a slim incessant
waterfall of notes like coins, until
he drops into grass, silent. This
pinnacle of air he mounts vertically,
swings upon through tall minutes
and vertically rocks down from, riding the currents,
is peaked, often as not,
too high to see.

So that rising near the zenith,
trailing
the trace of his largess
like a loose kitestring, he dwindles to
a black speck, a twinkle,
in the sky's wide eye:
to a dark star sparkling.

Search out the first pale
star some evening, then for an instant
look away. Like him, that star
may efface itself in vastness
and your eyes strain,
seeing only the motes within them swipe
across blue nothing,
to pick one point back out of nothing.

The twilight flight-song
the star-size skylark sings, vanishing
at the limit of your sight outstretched,
might be the star's.

Postscript: Confronted with Poe's "bird or devil" (if ever
he were), Walt Whitman might have remembered his
own "Demon or bird!" with much the same weird sink-
ing *I* felt, having just reread for the first time in, oh,
fourteen years: "The pale purple even / Melts around
thy flight; / Like a star of Heaven / In the broad day-
light / Thou art unseen, but yet I hear thy shrill delight
..." Freak coincidence? Or, worse, could Shelley's star
have lodged somehow in me, to burrow out in England
like a seventeen-year locust or an old bullet? Though
that image couldn't possibly have meant much till I'd
earned my own cricking neck and eyestrain headaches
trying to find a speck I'd lost in the sky, and found the
wishing star instead ... no, but Shelley must have done

it too! Suddenly I was positive: gazing up, up, some spring evening a century and a half ago, Shelley himself must have felt the little shock, the unexpected slippage and conjunction behind the eyes, even relief and gratitude like mine! Or put it this way: because I've done what Shelley did, just *as* he did it, I've seen the same one likeness, though he, because he was Shelley—found others, made rather more of the one, and of the skylark—made altogether more. But I, not Shelley, made this; and that's that.

THE GREENFLY QUESTION

A winter lethal to ladybirds did this.
In Lowestoft, they say, the pavements
have got too slippery to walk on, they're sweeping up
green heaps of the dead. Here
tourists who swarm these narrow streets
in numbers exceeded by greenflies alone

advance with grimaces, hands and papers flapping,
but remain upright. Yet the air's
a frenzy of winged aphids, double gnatsize,
that brush from hair and clothes like crumbs.
The whole surface of the sluggish brown Cam
is subtly flecked, the fish won't touch them,

the swallows can't be seen to, though
one eats one's fair share jogging.
A sweaty body swipes through flies
like a damp mop through dust;
an oiled nude sunbather is a vast
greenflypaper. After a while you wonder.

If roses and lime trees are the worse
for greenflies, crops are none. *We* don't
get stung or eaten in turn, just weakly
plentifully clung to. Yet
they're maddening—as if some monstrous
difficulty had been atomized to make

an atmosphere of purest aggravation.
Should we prefer our troubles
to niggle or address us? Which,
one gigantic rosetree-gobbling Greenfly
prowling the fens, or this mild trillionfold
minute one, second by second touching the skin like a hair?

SCATSQUALL IN SPRING

What salt sprinkled over half a ripe tomato
does to acid and red—
what sandpaper rasped over fingertips
does to the tumblers—

this squall of rain
swept like a sprinkling-can
over fields and pastures has done
to the smells of cut grass, riverwater, weedflowers,
turned clods and foddercrops, and to the superior
dung of graminivore:

on the paved footpath, bountiful green amoeba-splashes
(messy, though not offensive) of beefcow;
from the deep brown paddock,
intoxicating cloud of pony.

We Sunday ramblers,
canine and human, who watch our step
among these creatures now with pleasurably
twitching nostrils and no conscience to speak of,
might well feel mortified. We've dined,
and will again, upon the grass-gross haunches of their
    kind,
and know the muck they make of grass
is out of comparison nicer than the muck we make
of them,
of grass-in-them.

Like a slipped hound
a question circles, nose to the ground.

Ponder the rabbit-pellet whitetail,
the "flower-fed buffalo" with his fuel chips,
wildebeest, wapiti, wild ass; rehearse the natural habits of
the zebra, the slim pronghorn, the eland and the ibex,
and of the kudu.

Think how they live,
the ones you've seen—about the Zoo:
those dirt enclosures lacking one green blade,
that haybale diet (not Asian or African hay
even), and yet recall
how happily far
their dense organic odors are
above the stifling cathouse or
the house of apes and monkeys! There was a man ate grass
once, in the Bible, but it was madness.

A little tax
on brainpower? A little joke
at wits' expense?

Upside down in the gleaming river now
the elderly white pony, the chestnut, the roan,
gleam and crop grass.
A fresh breeze dries the fragrances
pouring off turf and blossom; and beyond the last stile
forty lowing Herefords with but a single thought
between them lope on joints of wood
to the pasture's watered lower end. As one
they lower ponderous heads
to graze. Stiffly, one by one, they raise
tails of frayed rope.

THE OLD COUNTRY
OLD WARDEN AERODROME

for Dave Woodley

As a child I sometimes had this dream.
I could fly. It was done
by rhythmic undulations, my sleeping body become
a thing of buoyancy and power—
the Icarus-dream all children surely dream,
soaring and falling. So Peter Pan; so
Nils aboard his goose. If later
this should endure and prove
the one dream, as it did for you,
there's the Air Force or private lessons;
flight is a dream
worth its weight in gold, but it comes true.

Now below a dome of turbulence I watch
an antique "aeroplane" made young again
bank above me. The pilot, in helmet and Red Baron scarf,
waves from the open cockpit. I
don't wave back, my heart refusing
to lift much even with those veteran wooden
wings, or wings of fabric-covered metal;
it positively quails as roaring
midgets called Gloster Gladiator and Fairey Swordfish
careen toward the spectators,
bright boxy toys saved
out of the dangerous childhood of aeronautics.

Fragile and intricate as boxkites,
awkward as boxkites, one by one the old planes
chug into the sky, make a few passes, bounce again

onto the turf. Dave, you called it poetry.
I strain to watch as you would, to perceive
as you would, as the watching crowd clearly perceives

the poetry of aircraft,
of flying machines. And can just about see
why, as machines go, these are charming
because, oh,
they're delicate and small, touchingly gawky
squared on their spraddling wheels,
are "living history," need near-obsolete skills
to fly, and *fly*—okay? And concentrating now
I'm almost getting a drift of something
more, akin to bicycles and sailboats,
a skimming oneness, pilot and craft and element
in single-human scale—

when ROWR the Hawker Tomtit's billowy exhaust
breaks over us, black choking.
Well, then—hang gliders? Not this coward ... no. It's
  gone,
the dream of flight. When next a Tiger Moth
sweeps four stiff wings
over the crowd—its name a poem, itself a perfect
poem preserved and clearly droned
in language foreign, martial, and romantic—
I have to tell it (and tell you) I can't
follow, a phrase or two
is all that sticks from the old country
I'd all but forgotten, Dave, when I met you.

"Cambridge University Swimming Club
No Public Access to River"

I

Members in their seventies fail to recall
a filthier July. Mildew rots the roses
before they open, the wet wind hurts. Finally,
so rarely, reprieve—dissolving turquoise sky
poured from a honeypot, a week's ration of summer
condensed in a day. This dazzling morning
the Club lures and subverts, druglike. Work?
How could any of us keep, or go, away?

At Sheep's Green, where the public swim,
shrieking bodies clog the numbing river;
boats hazard a way among them and pole upstream.
Picnic hampers, guitars. Half a mile and they'll
glide past our little greensward, their three or four
necks craning: a naughty glimpse of Eden! Adam
and Eve, though, are winding themselves in towels.
It might be Mrs. Grundy. It might be the Law.

Still, these rare aqua days, we grow careless.
Come ahead, boats. Too much bother, hastily
splashing out of the effervescent Cam
every couple of minutes and for what?
Deep under chestnut tassles and skeleton elms,
screened by rank goldenrod and a straggle of privet,
we sprawl on dandelions in bliss. The palest
sunshafts made us addicts; these suffuse us.

Again and again we rise and enter the river.

2

No punts in view, no paddlers? Good.
—Nip down four treads
Of weathered wood
And slime, and plunge away. I swim
Breast stroke carefully so my head's
Held out, above the dubious skim,

Perhaps of oil, like that on tea
Cooled in the pot.
Ahead, my vee-
Shaped strokes part flotsam: nameless muck
Stirred up by punt-poles from the bot-
tom, algae, sticks, leaves, petals. Yuck.

The winds that skim the surface clear
Elsewhere, fall foul
Of tall trees here.
Not for the squeamish, this. Indeed
I've more than once choked back a howl,
Clutched round the ankle by some weed.

But Cam feels lovelier than she looks
Close-to, and teeming
Swans and ducks,
Ducklings, cygnets, and schools of dace
Proclaim her waters safe for swimming
(If not for putting in your face).

This year the city's closed Sheep's Green.
"Admission Free,
Risk Yours" they mean,
Like cigarettes; yet what a throng!
Club stalwarts who with unfeigned glee
Take lunchtime dips all winter long

Don't die, what's more, and they *dive* in!
Time was, however . . .
Let's let Gwen
Raverat, Darwin grandchild, tell.
As an old lady, Mrs. Raver-
at could still "remember the smell

very well, for all the sewage went into the river, till the
town was at last properly drained, when I was about
ten years old. There is a tale of Queen Victoria being
shown over Trinity by the Master, Dr. Whewall, and
saying, as she looked down over the bridge: 'What are
all those pieces of paper floating down the river?' To
which, with great presence of mind, he replied: 'Those,
ma'am, are notices that bathing is forbidden.' However,
we lived at the upper end of town, so it was not so very
bad. That was why the bathing places were on the upper
river, on Sheep's Green and Coe Fen."

This was the 1890s. Gwen again:

3

"All summer, Sheep's Green and Coe Fen were pink
with boys, as naked as God made them; for bathing
drawers did not exist then; or, at least, not on Sheep's
Green. You could see the pinkness, dancing about, quite
plain, from the end of our Big Island. Now to go Up
the River, the goal of all the best picnics, the boats had
to go right by the bathing places, which lay on both
sides of the narrow stream. These dangerous straits were
taken in silence, and at full speed. The Gentlemen were
set to the oars—in this context one obviously thinks of
them as Gentlemen—and each Lady unfurled a parasol,
and, like an ostrich, buried her head in it, and gazed
earnestly into its silky depths, until the crisis was past,
and the river was decent again."

—if only they'd do it now, what a lot of trouble
all concerned would be saved! the bathers who, cursing,
must scoot for cover each time another flat prow
pushes beyond the bend; the sad little flasher
who climbs the fence and crackles in the bushes
waiting to prance out, madly waving his penis,
at the first boat with a woman aboard; the woman,
her outing spoiled, who then must file a complaint;
the policeman who must cycle down here, take names,
try to arrest somebody; and the boaters
fled from, thwarted, never allowed to ogle—

though businessmen, clerks, writers, dons and students,
laborers, civil servants, engineers,
one archeologist, one librarian, and,
on really nice days, the tart old Dean of Pembroke,
stretched out on towels, small piles of clothes beside them,
napping, chatting, busy with books and papers,
sixty-year age span, scrawny to fit to fat,
naked of course (not counting glasses), otherwise
too ordinary for words and nearly all male—
a company which relaxes and delights me
as none has yet—should be ogled a certain way . . .

4

Each
is personal as a thumbprint.
Soon, you know your friends' exactly
the way you know
their eyes, or hands, or height.

Whenever the elusive sun
shines, a flower-garden profusion
blooms mid-daily here, a lush display
of lolling Roman limbs and unconfinement, filling
the gaze, so rich and various,
so much to see

48

and everywhere in motion:
wobble of standing
languid fishflop of rolling-over
cumbrous swing of striding.
A subtle thickening, lengthening, relapsing
tones our companionship,

and the riveting changes
gravity and pushups ring on what was lately
shriveled in the cold river
were waked by idle talk
in what's now quarter-inching darkly
along a sunflushed thigh in curls,
slowly pulling a sweater on over its head.

I'm fascinated.
This garden-variety talent ever
seems a form of true
sorcery, some part held in common by
the bottled djinn, Clark Kent in public, the werewolf
under the new moon:
shape-shifters,
their powers in check; the changing prodigious,

the changing back no less.

Unassumingly, a shaftless button
cloaks a dagger. Oh, but
look! For now the cloak slits open,
the dagger slides thrillingly in its sheath . . .

Yet because we're so
precarious really, safe together only
within a membrane
too easily torn and just beneath eggshell, because
we mutually acknowledge
this, without words,

the subject of Danish films or Dutch beaches
is dropped. Almost unseen
pulses had quickened, but not much.
Beneath my skin
a tiny buzzing vibrator had begun
its friendly nuzzling, but does not
insist.

So we subside in sunshine. Truly,
this is bliss:
to bask here, daisy amid sunflowers,
strand among other strands
in a plain web of titillation and trust,
noticing everything, agreeably
nattering on about politics—work—food—
the filthy weather, no summer this year . . .

WHINNY MOOR CROSSING

*The belief in Yorkshire was amongst
the vulgar (perhaps is in part still)
that after the person's death the
soule went over Whinny-Moore . . .*
                    John Aubrey, 1686

. . . she loved thee, cruel Moor . . .
                    Emilia to Othello

Unable to crackle, trying not to tear,
the swollen map unfolds. Rain pelts it.
Its thin intelligent lines squirm:
blue stream, brown contours. Here
as I'd remembered are
the standing stones, the "Cross (remains of),"
the marked Way; surely then that ridge
(dialect: rigg) ascends in shades of tan
just here, beyond a stream (beck), which ought to be
this stream, Grain Beck. But where on paper
red dashes stitch a footpath
down to the beck and slantwise up,
soaked heather snarls round my knees
unbroken but by a maze of sheeptracks.
My path went along and failed
and the heather closed in. And here I am.

Somewhere not far, but where? The downpour pours
drearily on, rinses my face numb, leaks past
my hood's tight drawstring, a water
continuous with the ragged sky trailing the ground
of noplace I can fix; and while I look round perplexed
the fog (roke) thickens like a pudding.
I know, I've read, how chilled a body
this weary gets

how fast in weather this foul,
and that to some of those lost on the moor-tops,
able to find no spot not sodden, nothing
to shelter under or behind, or make a fire with,
death comes down with darkness. From both shoulders
where the pack's jaws have closed
a tedious keening rises; but this—
a handful of raisins and a drink—
is all I can do about it. Let me *think*.

Compass deep in the backpack camel's hump
under this loop'd and window'd nylon poncho,
is anything you could tell me worth a worse drenching?
Either beck this might be flows north, says Map.

Bugwit Herdwick, comfy in oily wool,
mournfully bleating out of the green wastes
like a poor lost soul, your supper's under your nose,
your feet aren't freezing. Who's a stray sheep? Not you.

Wit be my sheepskin now ... but pictures
keep crowding in: Lord Peter Wimsey
sinking, on a night of sudden fog,
neck-deep in a Yorkshire bog; being
held up by Bunter; being dragged out like a cork
with ropes; ah, and that feckless villain
in flight from Sherlock Holmes, with none to save him,
perishing offstage in another fogbound mire
on deepest Dartmoor (who'd save me, pray?) ...
image of Catherine Linton's pitiful ghost
that lost its way on the moor
and wandered there for twenty years,
its icy fingers rapping at last, beyond the casement
its child's face floating ...
all around is Brontë country, where
the wind's verb is wuther, where centuries out of mind

a woman would come to funerals and sing
an eerie song, I know, slow, in a minor key:

This ae nighte, this ae nighte,
  —Every nighte and alle,
Fire and fleet and candle-lighte,
  And Christe receive thy saule.

When from hence away art past,
  —Every nighte and alle,
To Whinny-muir thou com'st at last

And Christ receive thy soul.
The Lyke Wake Dirge—see *leich* or *lik*, a corpse.

No. Keep your head. Moorland is like the sea,
like jungle hearts-of-darkness, forests primeval, deserts
Saharan, Arctic, Himalayan. These
compel as much as chill us. They are the Earth
raised like a barrow to a rare power
that baffles reason and stupefies it, leaving fantasy
to account, by myth and Gothic tale, for whatever
happens in there, out there ... which doubtless explains
why *I*—footsore, cold, wet, worried, alone
and given to the moor against my will—even now
might almost be beginning to sense
the iron gates between factual and fantastic
unfastening in the fog.
                              For buried
high in cloud, the world rubbed out,
how weirdly plausible seem, all of a sudden,
the Yorkshire madwife in the attic,
the small hirsute "Hob-men" and witch-hags
once so thick hereabouts that my guidebook
mentions by name and deed, of all those still remembered,
only the most notorious. Wait—
don't *I* remember

53

how wraiths of moor-mist wisped round the Wolfman
snarling on tipclaw through the Gypsy wagons
to maul his girlfriend?
                            —imagination surprised
in guilty acts of obeisance—terrified,
infatuated—before a fell power old beyond thought.
The very peat sopping underfoot   *If ever*
feels dense with a peopled past, not fibers
merely   *thou gav'st hos'n and shoon*   but
passions of those who once lived
familiar among forces I can scarcely suppose at,
and don't   *Sit thee down and put them on*   don't
in the least want to! *If hos'n and shoon*
thou ne'er gav'st nane The whinnes sall prick
To harry such dead as these
across the moor, how credible, how fitting
The whinnes sall prick thee to the bare bane
And Christe receive thy saule

—Barefoot through gorse and ling the lost soul stumbles,
sobbing with pain and cowardice and regret
if not remorse. The sweet thick gorse-musk sickens it,
long gorse-spines prick its feet to the bare bone,
pale gorse-flowers glimmer. Limping, whimpering, gagging,
it passes over the wastes of moor-gorse (whins).

In fog and rain, night closing, what moor
is not a Whinny Moor, what Whinny Moor
isn't a state of mind? To pass this night out here . . . !

And right here's where you pull yourself together.

Packet and flask slip back into packpockets; zip
and zip. Right: the roke looks possibly paler now,
the map is what there is to go by. Decide to trust it;
go where you must as if a path led there.

The tough stems gnarling their talons: elude them;
the little dark implacable leaves: lunge through,
pluck up your mudball boots, *dressage*, come over.
Spot sheeptracks and go streamward when they do
as with a blundering current; flounder—
portable hunchback tent with porthole—over
the beck and struggle up
straight through the rigg's opposing heather tangle,
its hanks of snagged filthy fleece,
its heartlurch grouse grenades bursting
under your bootsoles of stout Vibram
no thorn can pierce: endure these too:
climb on. Smokily gulping, always out of wind
entirely, poncho whipping in wind that never will
run out, that nothing's broken for miles
and miles of closegrown open treeless folded roundness
fog-obscured yet ever-sensible, climb, climb

until the sky
lifts and condenses and the world below you
blows open like a wet map, faded, soundless; and *there*
up and ahead, tracing the rigg's long spine,
a trail one glance at the map in hand
explains:
                    miscalculation, costing
hours, mud, hills, later a loose bull also; but now
no lion-size flame-slavering hound,
no mired pony's screams,
no high wail—name of a lover—
draining away in gooseflesh, nothing like that
and nothing worse. So at the end to lie
beatific, warm, landlocking radiant
soup and tea under the hostel roof
unburdened, bootless, dry socks, sagging cot, six blankets

make now the long mite-march down the camel's hump:
a mangy heath-shag scratched thin in patches
of brilliant bracken, or bald in ashpale
burnover (swidden), down either flank, falling away below.
Heather sweep upon sweep—subtle
purples and reds under the vast dead green,
orange soaked from stems the wet wuthering
moves through but hardly moves. Rain
thins, sky lightens. Where I am
I know, and where I'm going; and where I've been
I'll not forget, nor how to get there again.

THREE

Settling

FOR TED

WILL

The tamer, straining all his nerve and skill,
Keeps Panic hunkered on her pedestal,

Makes Jealousy the leopard leap through flame,
The panther Fury slope along the beam

Like any backfence tom with massive feet,
And Terror burst a paper hoop, and Hate

Rise supple in his gaudy stripes to beg
Then shoulder down, a rolled-up tiger rug.

Or not quite: if that fierce attention blinks
All spring. Beneath his shirt are scars like staves
His props—the whip, chair, pistolful of blanks—
Could not forestall, and ugliest are Love's.
Like stone his stare when Love's exploding din
Slams through the Big Top's shapely dome of bone.

Reaching Around

(For Walt Whitman)

I have perceiv'd that to be with those I like is enough ...
To pass among them or touch any one, or rest my arm ever so
lightly round his or her neck for a moment, what is this
then?
I do not ask any more delight, I swim in it as in a sea.

1972

We're all uproarious, Philip and I and his
preposterously pregnant wife who can't get up,
their sofa's sagged too low, just since yesterday
she's too immense—or tired, it's late,
I should think about rising, but for me as well
that's hard. Harder each time in fact
to leave this house, though on the carpet I'm
dissembling more and more: for the past hour
I've been aware, as mercifully they're not
yet, of the slow ache secretly uncoiling
down the long inner muscles of my arms,
clamped round me for safe-keeping. I can visualize
these muscles, as in a Ben-Gay ad,
spangled to show the pain. The pain bears lengthwise
down, bears down, bears down; my elephantine
friend, hilarity-weakened, tries again to heave
herself out of her seat, it's her they want
mostly, she's great, who wouldn't? Shhh don't don't

Driving home I sober up at once.
The outlook's awful, instinct says not a prayer.
At arm's length sure, they like me, I can feel it,
but the least whiff of serious weirdness—oh,
damn the damn thing! clumsily complicating

what should be unaffected, plain ... poor arms,
they want to reach around, that's all, an impulse
so natural it's cruel to have to inhibit,
so mulish it's exhausting to, and so
imperative it's freakish. Don't I know.

1955

Scout camp at twelve. Through sunburned weedfields
my group of girls kicks tentward. Grasshoppers
explode about us, our shirts and shorts, and limbs,
accumulate those smaller leaf-green hopping
things that live in tall weeds in Ohio.
A prickly walk, I like it, glad to be
one among them at this ugliest age
of inch-thick glasses, nose and sailor hat
and mammoth chest, and so forth. So I've got
my copious third period now—so what!
To my mind I'm no Girl, I'm just plain Scout.

We're telling what we're going to be; I volunteer
"A missionary to Africa." Touched by this,
our nicest counselor, Margie, slides a half-hug
round my stiff shoulder. For me to shrug
from under growling "Mush!" is automatic,
I really have to, yet in a trice I'm dying
to take back both: her arm, my churlish gesture—
unthinkable. We both feel bad.
I scuff on, blazing trail through prickly heat,
Queen Anne's lace, bugs on springs, all trussed up tight
in a self-image, Billy Goat Gruff's own Kid.

1968

A stone-cold toad-hideous
gargoyle squats on a sofa   croaking   croaking
warts all blood ...
aghast, my friends strip beds,

61

pile covers on, but nothing warms
or comforts, or shuts me up: *Be physical
with kids*, obsessively. The parents
behold my state in wonderment, confer in whispers;
their little boy, who's two,
runs in circles endlessly,
hollering till nerve-ends
squirm gibbering through lumpy skin, while I
don't stop and don't stop
hoarsely warning his macho dad: hold him, cuddle him.
Often as I've since been thanked
for this advice, or order, I still marvel
it was heeded. "You
kidding? The envoy from the brink of doom? My God,
that shaking voice, those cold thin fingers
clutching every blanket in the house
around you—you had authority,
believe me, I *believed* you."

   1963

Classic Hall, mid-evening and mid-May.
I'm nominally reading in "my" office
but concentration's poor. Far down along
the dark corridor, light squares through a doorframe—
my teacher-mentor-"father," working late.
How soon can I go calling? Wait.
Don't crowd. Studying him closer than Shakespeare,
his ease, warmth, gentleness, his . . . anti-Gruffness,
I've glimpsed some happier ways to be not spineless
than Dad's. A mild and passive missionary,
he thinks I *go at* things too hard. (He would.)
Well, fine—I'll be his auto-convert

                                             Light
snaps out, spatter of rubber footsteps—*wait!*
Slam book, grab notes and pen, pelt headlong down
the black stairs, catch him up too breathless—Hi!

I just this minute finished *Henry the Fifth*!
Isn't that last act awful? Courtly love—
Catharine—"God of battles"—Falstaff/Hal—
The door; revealing racket muted against
a close, soft, honeysuckle-hyperbolic
Hoosier spring night. Between two breaths I'm offered
a lift back to the dorm. "Sure, thanks a lot!"
On flows and flows the babbling brook of language,
undammable   we're halfway to the car
his sudden warm enclosing hand   his voice
a chuckle   mine a plug-jerked radio

1979

Whitman, when I read over what you wrote
I have to wonder. Takes one to know one, right?
You doted on yourself, there was that lot of you
and all so luscious; you found no sweeter fat
than stuck to your own bones. Oh yeah?
No doubts then? It's our weakness to confuse
wish and conviction, ought-to-be with is,
and something in your voice ... but if I'm wrong
and you aren't bluffing, Walt, how happy you were
in that belief. I'm mired, I'm pretty sure,
in doubt for keeps. It creeps and creeps along,
a glacial progress I extrapolate
will have me hugging friends, age 68,
in 2010; I don't call that a cure.

The touch that heals? The laying on of hands?

When (in 1970) on the Delaware
I was the Scout camp counselor,
not for the first time nor the last, we had
this problem child. Obnoxious fat complainer,
she hated camp, crafts, swimming, cookouts, hikes—
Ready to brain the brat, I overheard

63

Margaret, my assistant, remark offhand
as if to state the obvious, "That kid
just needs to be held and held." Dumb stare: she did?
I of all people had the least excuse
not to sense that. And hugging her felt *good*,
how can I put this right? almost as though
that thistly girl were me at her age, ten—
as though my reflex fendings-off had been
taken for what they were, and been ignored.

Balky, sulky, stiff in my arms as wood,
what was her name? *She*'d be in college now,
that camper who alone could tell us what
came of our cuddling—anything? If not
enduringly for her, to me it's meant
ever since then—that no child's need
gnarl into mine unmet—I've been released
to reach toward children every way one can,
help them be certain, clear to the marrow-lattice,
the fat that sticks to their bones is sweeter than sweet,
self-evident as weight and sight, so they
may never in their lives endure self-loathing
or self-constraint because of "a few light kisses,
a few embraces, a reaching around of arms"
that didn't happen. Otherwise no—except
as, clustered in a beaten space between
peaked huts, Kikuyu watch a white fanatic's
kind, sweaty, earnest face, or classroomful
of undergraduates sits forward rapt—

for who's the missionary *alias*
professor now, who strains to touch and change
minds with a mind? (I never saw this, strange—
language as sublimated touch, ideas
as sublimated—something . . .) Yet despite
that half-truth, and how stirring it can be

to touch a book and seem to touch a man,
flesh that embraces flesh still satisfies
our childish fat-and-bones' avidity
better than "Crossing Brooklyn Ferry" can
—though you were right.

Envoy

Whoever I am holding you now in hand,
I've understood how much that luscious lot
You rightly said you were would understand
This long hug made of words that say I'm not.

WALK WITH THE RIVER

Iowa City

A southbound current, strong,
Littered with leaves, slides beside me.
I'm keeping even.
It's October. On the bank ahead
a cardinal lights high in a maple tree.
I pass the tree. It blazes, in it
the bird blazes, through it
the sky is indigo; it's afternoon . . .

A good child
gets taken for a walk. She wears
brown shoes and a sweater,
holds her father's hand and looks
again and again to him,
only to him:
the powerful, patient, steady one
who—going someplace—
brings her along partway.
He is preoccupied but kind.
In his mind the entire route is plain.
She holds his hand. They go along
not speaking; but each time she looks
she is reassured.

Now they come south together,
through the park. Any minute now
he'll recollect himself
and send her back; she eyes
the burnished buckeyes
but lets them lie. Carefully
her shoes crunch leaves. A red bird,
burning, flies into a red tree;
they pass the tree.

The Spellbinding

Then by all means, the baker said,
Step in and help yourself. My bread?
Sea-salt and honey, flour and yeast,
Dab of shortening, cold distilled
Water, and seasonings to taste—
Not everyone's of course! He smiled

Politely, dusted floury hands.
Smooth crusts lay cooling in some pans;
Bulging from its bowl, a batch
Of dough puffed on the pilot light,
Working, alive. He let me watch
Him pummel all the yeast gas out,

Flapping and kneading, sprinkling flour—
Fingers', wrists', joy-dance of power,
Motion and form in beauty blent . . .
I bit, chewed twice: astonishment,
Shock, even rapture! Stout and proud
The oven breathed a hot sweet cloud.

No change forever. Here I stay
Spell-bound in this bakery.
The baker, like his bread, is good;
He minds, but gives me what he can.
The staff of life! For gratitude
I strive to live by bread alone,

But every morsel touts his skill
And stupidly my weak eyes fill.
I can't break loose, or learn or quit—
Oh baker, what a fool I feel!
I've tried, it isn't possible;
I can't distinguish you from it.

Mezzo Cammin

I

I mean to mark the Midway Day
With soundings in this verse-form. Say,
        Muse, how you hate it!
I know your taste for excess. But
These jingly rhymes must undercut,
        Counter, deflate it.

I trust them, and I can't trust you
To practice self-restraint. In lieu
        Of building
Some Watts Tower to my fulcrum age
I've shut you in this little cage;
        Start gilding!

The stanzas should be varied slightly,
Thus: some more and some less tightly
        Nipped at the waist
And ankles, odd lines fitting an extra s-
yllable in, or with a dextrous
        Flick of the wrist

Some rhymes set slant, and so forth; still
It's tight, you'll have to try, Muse. Trill
        Like a canary,
Bright jailbird, swing your wee trapeze!
Come come, don't sulk. Laudamus, please—
        Not miserere.

2

At 21, by now, what did
I want/expect? At least one kid,
    More like a triad;
The man; to've written books in whose
Thickets a troubled child could lose
    Itself, as I had.

Might I have made a kid-glove fit
Of wifery and kiddy lit
    And being Mother—
Slipped chipper as a Chinese foot
Stunted into my doll-size boot—
    Or sensed I'd smother

And howling burst the seams—or ripened
Like a summer squash? It's happened;
    The odd wife sprouts
In marriage as in fertilizer.
Single, shall I grow full-size, or ... ?
    Doubts or no doubts,

"The family experience"—
Engrossing, commonplace; one's chance
    To mother better
Than Mother did—I've missed that; I'm
Too old, now, to begin in time
    At last. A matter

I hope will come to matter less,
Though there's no question childlessness
    Bears harder
Than spinsterhood. Since all the strong
Kind types go off the market young,
    It's murder

To find one single, able, willing,
Sane, and minimally appealing
    Body/work/wit;
But there's still *time*. "Too old" 's what's poignant.
Only one other disappointment
    Overpowers that:

Losing the Baptists: wash of grief.
(A hamstring harped-on loud enough
    Already.)
Not even Jesus, Ethicist
Survives this far; if not the Christ,
    Nobody.

O *Kinder, Kirche*, let me go,
How can I bless you now? I know,
    I trust, the center
That holds, holds more than family
And faith, and warms a place for me
    In bleak mid-winter.

   3
Start Spinster Lib? We spinsters pull
Up stakes and fly to Istanbul
    On low-cost charters!
Of the past ten, I've wangled three
Years foreign. And mobility
    Is just for starters:

Spinsters who spend the night don't phone;
Spinsters go trekking on their own
    And have a swell time.
One, on a solitary jaunt,
Comes close to people couples don't,
    Glued in the birdlime

Of one another's omnipresence.
—Fresh views, late talk, warmth; tumescence
       Also (which thrives
On talk) unlooked-for, not surprising,
Nice. Nice way of improvising
       Alternate lives.

Then, after breakfast, off you go. It's
No bad thing for "nature poets"
       To solo through.
Though hiking with a friend is splendid,
Hike got less of me than friend did
       When one came too.

In every sense you're more acute
Alone. You note what's what en route,
       You're not distracted.
Plus (irony) so long as you're
Abroad upon the tumbling moor
       Where Life's enacted—

So perilous, so gorse-gilt, so
Abundant—friendships seem godsent.
       Always, you're shaken—
Joy is a shock; you're . . . *reverent*.
By tough old maid wayfarers no
       True friend gets taken

For granted, nor do loving's other
Faces blear through custom either.
       Spinsters have learnt
To value what they can't get used to—
Values many a wife's reduced to,
       Wishing she weren't!

Too cramped, she envies (irony)
Us bachelor girls, so long less free
      Than outcast! Yearning
To spread roots in a roomy plot,
We crumpled them into some pot
      And went sojourning.

The life abroad calls into question
Style, assumptions Yank and Christian,
      Habits (how you
"Two-handed engine"?—fork your plateful);
Forces thought and choice. I'm grateful.
      The road from Lou-

isville to Lund was passing strange
But now I'm through I wouldn't change,
      Cresting my peak age,
For kids and home. A Lu:uhv'le shut
Mind, close and smoky as a hut,
      Came with that package.

Things have the disadvantages,
It's claimed, of their advantages—
      Of light and air, then.
I think so. No one gets it all.
The grass is green here too; I call
      My draw a fair one.

Two Curios

I. JANUARY STARLINGS, SINGING

*(After a Lyric Stanza-Form
by Edna St. Vincent Millay, Found in Her Poem
"The Poet and His Book")*

Sing, you starlings, sing!
Winter's at the middle,
Seven weeks till Spring—
Hurry things a little!
Week-old snow is still around
Soiled and sagging at the edges;
Birdsong in the woods and hedges,
Winter on the ground.

Though you've been beguiled,
Mixing up your seasons
Since the morning's mild,
Or for subtler reasons,
When some voice within you sings
Suddenly with certain vision,
Let it say with all decision
Winter's name or Spring's.

Call it what you choose;
You can make the choices.
If the greens and blues
Of your clamorous voices
Paint the Spring, then well they may:
Winter is a way of thinking
With a quill pen, India-inking
Stiff black lines on gray.

73

Starlings, I don't care.
Let the world awaken
While you sing out there,
Instinctual but mistaken.
For the song is quick and clear,
For the leafless branch would hold you
Just as lightly if I told you
You should not be here.

2. UNICORN

*(After Stephen Vincent Benét
and Vachel Lindsay)*

A child was conjured, and walked the strand
Feeling her childhood seep in sand—
Nearly all gone now—stiff with dread
Of life when wonder and love are dead.
The flint moon reeled like a broken wheel
And cold sparks sprayed from a sea like steel
About her; shivery, rapt, she came
Breathing the wind while the moon made flame
Run on the waves. It was grief and bliss:
Help me! Let me not lose all this!

What made it happen? The surf broke free,
The moon burned liquid; out on the sea,
Gathered of light and spray, was born
A dream-thing bearing a single horn
Of light, and she knew him: the Unicorn.

Fidgeting, dancing on air and foam
He poised there, checked in a fury of speed,
Moon-colored, tide-colored, mercury, chrome.
The pride of his neck was a god's indeed—
The dark wind tangled his mane and tail—

74

Oh, he seemed Life then, and Joy, and Grace,
Kept for the instant, but flexed to race,
His forelegs trampling the sea in place,
Tendons of cable, feet like a flail!

"I ran and shouted and sobbed for breath
While the waves strove whitely against the shore,
Wait for me, wait while they raged toward death
And struck at the gale with a fuming roar;
And the flint moon melted to ivory,
And my ears went thick with the bump of blood,
For still in that simmering light he stood.
His shoulders and flanks gone snowcloud-hued
He stood like an ice-beast, looking at me.

The moment lengthened; he stopped the night.
He stopped my hurtling. I saw or sensed
The neat hooves braced at the brink of flight,
The comber beneath them gathered and tensed,
The stars spiked fast to the windscoured skies,
The smooth moon, lopsided, dropped to west,
The surf curled down in a frozen crest;
And the painful gasping stopped in my chest
While the long look shuddered between our eyes.

Then he flowed, and spun, and leapt for the light,
And nothing was left on the sea but night."

The surf seethed toward her. She wailed and fell;
I've lost him—lost—I'm lost like a knell
Tolled in her head till she flailed the sand,
Answered and lost. On the empty strand
The emptier ocean broke and broke,
And the froth said: *Lossst.* And the child awoke
To colorless breakers, a gritty beach,
The dream forever beyond her reach.

75

The moon's cold fire may burn and burn,
But never that girl at childhood's close
By fleetness, or craft, or courage, learn
To mount the Unicorn; this she knows.
Now all of her hope is memory.
Not for an age will his horn be let
In her lap instead, and she mourns him yet,
And mourning, believes, and will never forget
The lovely, pitiless thing on the sea.

Found Poems

(Note: In most species and pairs, and under most circumstances, only the male songbird sings.)

I. THE TYPE

When female Song Sparrows   sing
it is usually
in the period before nest-building. They utter

short   unmusical   songs

from higher perches
                    than females
                                        normally
choose. One such
female
wandered from male to male

and was
unduly long in laying
the first egg. Birds of this   type

are unusually aggressive . . .

The song may be
'very loud' and is like
the adult male's with all the music and variety

omitted.

2. BIG BUT

When female
song   is uttered only by
exceptional
females, it practically always

differs
to some extent
from the male's song

but
in other species
in which female song is
usual . . .
the songs of the sexes

are indistinguishable.

3. IT HAPPENS

Males
sometimes approach singing females, apparently
puzzled by their behavior.

The mate of such a bird may become
confused
and attack her.

4. TEXTBOOK CASE

Occasional females may
sing   a little
and yet be sufficiently
normal
to rear a brood.

One such female
                    stopped
singing
after laying the third egg . . .

At this nest the cock
undertook
major responsibility for
feeding the young and sanitation.

He spent much time
chevying
            his mate to   her
                                        duties . . .

5. CONDITIONAL

It would
seem   that sometimes
lack of normal
        sexual
        activity   may
evoke exceptional song from female

birds

KEY WEST
(TRIPLE BALLADE WITH ENJAMBED REFRAIN,
PLUS ENVOY)

for David Jackson

The garden's shading. Let there be
Tea in the deck-and-louvre tent
Begun, degree by slow degree,
Upon its languid, smooth descent
Toward eighty. Rose and succulent
Look up from blooming peatbeds thick
With strangeness, lush, ebullient
Displayed against white-sand-and-brick

Paving. From frond to shrub to tree
(So *that's* what Orphan Annie meant!)
Lizards are leaping—skittery,
Dirt-colored, slim, belligerent,
Each furnished with a prominent
Accessory featured in their shtick,
Unvocal, yet grandiloquent
Displayed against white sand and brick.

Say X has accidentally
Invaded turf big Z has spent
His little life defending: Z
Does jerky push-ups, does Present
Throat-Flap (inflated? through a vent?),
Out-in, out-in, erotic tic
Of warning—Pounce! and *skitter* went
Displayed-Against. White sand and brick

Are not much less intelligent,
Frankly. They'll "flap" a leaf or stick,
Bright membrane flashing Go! Repent!
Displayed against white sand and brick.

The reptile brain is cold and small,
No space, no need for judgment there.
Watch. In the deepest Turtle Kraal
A monstrous head pokes up for air,
Lairpet of Grendel's, chased from lair
To scare up dinner. Jaws of dread
Gasp open. Eyes of earthenware
Identify. The loggerhead

Lunges on cue; the guide will trawl
A chunk of rotten lobster where
He'll strike. Abruptly I recall
The moth aflutter on the bare
Floorboards, the little lizard's stare,
Fixed, from the threshold, how it sped
Across the varnish . . . yes. Compare?
Identify? the loggerhead

Who wallows, tries to climb the wall,
Whose ton of crushing-power can tear
A man in chunks and eat him all,
Whose fins thrash up the mal de mer,
Who now, with all that force to spare,
Crushes the bait and sinks like lead.
A blonde child shrieks. These kinds of scare
Identify the loggerhead

And lizard with its charming flare
Round as a flannel tongue and red.
Look long, think well before you dare
Identify the loggerhead.

A green iguana spined with plates
Blinks at the tourist with a ques-
tion not these flattened welterweights':
Where are the dinosaurs of yes-
ter-Age? New Zealand and Loch Ness,
Pygmy Iguanodon, poor thing.
That clockwork, kneejerk, passionless
Instinct persists, but Reason's king.

It's Sophosaurus rex who baits
The sea-troll Instinct now. I guess
I'm glad—though how he tolerates
That filthy pool—! (As Freud would stress,
Whatever dragon we repress
Befouls its prison.) Evening
Brings us to ours, we both undress,
Instinct persists . . . but Reason's king

Here where a white bar melts, and spates
Of filtered water effervesce,
Pure azure balm that liquidates
Disturbing thoughts, the turtle mess,
The saurian heat, the—   S.O.S.?
Again? This same dumb lizardling
Keeps trying, with the same success—
Instinct persists (but Reason's king

Or else)—to scale the tiles. Noblesse
Oblige, a royal palm's frayed wing
Retrieves him from a giantess.
Instinct persists but Reason's king.

These trinkets, David—waterslick
Pool tiling, tiny splayfeet spread
On surface tension (rhetoric?),
Sea monster in his muckbath fed
On rot, display in tropicbed—
All thanks to you. The length of string
They're threaded on is only thread:
Instinct-persists-but-Reason's-king.

EINE KLEINE NACHTMUSIK

1

Stars on stalks
sparse in a vast field.
A sickle-blade of ice, the moon
has launched its slicing swing
largo. Where
the swath will happen,
starseeds tense to spring *allegro*
up, already blooming.

2

Easter Eve's
horizon glows in one place.
Off the Jersey coast
the bloody moon-yolk bulges *adagio*
up from the pushing sea.

Variations on a Theme

Even in pain you listen. *Watch* they say,
Like this. You nearly can, the new ones grow
So huge so quickly. On the patio
Each noon a patchier sunshine fights its way
Through webs of leaves held blade by famished blade
Taut to the light, repeating raptly: *Green.*
The wind is subtler; treetops shift between
Thrust and attainment, leaving you in shade.

Hurry they shout: these crowns of shadow dense
With us, our lives, will starve you; shade means die!
—Foreshortened, late, a season's almost over
Whose close will see that massy eloquence
Of foliage overspread and close the sky,
Shunting the sunlight somewhere else forever.

2. THE MYRTLE WARBLER

My window gave a startled thump; my heart
Thumped louder, certain what would flop or bunch
Below it. No. An arborvitae branch
Had reached out flat and low to intercept
The little trembling flattened bird, that gaped
And panted like a sprinter. Damn. Some cat
Would get her, something must have snapped—a bone,
Her nerve . . . yet soon she seemed much more alert,
Could turn her small sleek head, blink, watch me fret.
When I got home from jogging she was gone.

But where? How? Did the impact paralyze
Or only stun her; was mere time enough
To heal her of that violent surprise?
The pane, still perfect, wears a scrap of fluff.

"You hardly ever need to state *your feelings.
The point is to feel and keep the eyes open.
Then what you feel is expressed, is mimed back
at you by the scene. A room, a landscape. I'd
go a step further. We don't* know *what we feel
until we see it distanced by this kind of
translation."*

—James Merrill in an interview

A wet rough wall. A frothy bladed green
Lit from within; a slick, infernally glowing
Green restlessness. Stoked through a week of rain,
Cool chemical fires power the obsessive growing
That overfills my window frame with pain—
Too quick, too rank, too *green*! No way of knowing
By heart's hysteria or reeling brain
What hurts so much; instinctively I'm showing
Myself my forest, lush, aglow in gloom,
Whose tulip poplars soar through condensation,
Masts in a mist; whose great oak limbs assume
The shapes of Navajo prayer and Fifth Position.
It listens, breathes—incessant drip and steam
Of jungles—while in anguish or elation,
Eighty feet up, the crows and grackles scream
And thrash the branches, brainless, pure emotion . . .

Look to the greenwood, what you really feel
Glows back at you, the green light nets a knowledge
And hands the catch to Reason. Mind that so
Believes in its stern duty to control,

If not these feelings, what I finally do
With them, lies open to the bristling foliage,
To pheasants stalking loud and bright as parrots
Through honeysuckle, chatter of treetop squirrels
That leaping flick wet monkeytails in curls,
Enormous weeds like cabbages and carrots
Grown inches overnight, grown menacing—
Knows love, then doubt, then dread, of everything.

FAMILY PLANNING

since feeling is first
who pays any attention
to the syntax of things
will never wholly kiss you:
e. e. cummings

Before that single sperm,
nucleic bomb and blueprint, bursts
headlong through—
imploding its tiny world, changing
my world forever—
whose
and *when* and *why* will have been beforehand
judged with strict sense. I
have devised meanwhile
of rubber and coiled wire
a deadly baffle
for unelect sperm-hordes to bang
their noses on.
Oblivious of those hurtling teeming legions
beyond the poisoned
rampart, one
frumpish moonstruck princess after another
sleepwalks to her death
unrescued, incomplete. But soon
to one such urgent army
it must at last be given to breach
the pass and find
their moon-round sister. Whose kiss
shall wake her then,
and make her whole, and wholly beautiful?
Not for mere joy, nor gesture, no,
nor selfish love itself

may that fierce choice
be taken or be blessed. Hope
wrings hard in us,
its death is wretched. Yet when the froth-borne
missiles, heading home, home
on the ripe planet, ahead
rock-firm must stand decisions
righteous and wise. Then let there be
Life, and then
only: the sire good, careful, the day
a keen clear day.

Missing Person

for James Merrill

"You mean," said Andy, "that you gave birth to a ghost?"
Nonplussed for a second ("gave *birth*"?), I said I had.
Scowling, he shook his head, a longish head
Shaped like a lightbulb: "When?" I vaguely guessed

A "ghost" was a personal pet-thing that could fly,
Tinker Bell tricked out in a little sheet.
You rode your bike—the ghost, like a parakeet,
Rode you, or sailed along in the air nearby—

That much I'd gathered from Andy's attitude
Toward *his* ghost. Anyway, I coveted one.
"Last night," I hazarded. Hindsight opens again
The Real Book of Puppets and *Magic Made*

Easy, scissors and paints; it perceives in this
Casper-like ghost conception—friendly, small,
Invisible yet wholly in his control—
An elegant if unconscious synthesis

Of Andy's passions. Were all mine learned from him
But Tarzan, stargazing, reading (and writing verse:
"The thunderstorm races / Like horses with wings,
It cries out a warning / To all living things.")?
Some, like the ghost, he grudged me. He did worse.
A paragon lost can fix the paradigm

For a life; and ghost tales get to be parables.
Whose worth is measureless, his loss is sure.
By choice by chance by change shall you endure
A host of unendurable farewells

And fly about the world: depart depart!
(The angst is worse, and the world about to fly
Apart more surely, each time I move now—why?)
—A boy's face, scowling, relenting, galls the heart

He woke but kept on sufferance, happier
Than it could realize, never in graver peril . . .
Now Love and Loss—*your* burden, Mr. Merrill—
Drift through the haunted house of who we were.

It beggars reason, how one bright runt I last
Laid eyes on at eleven should persist
So bright in memory that I'll still go by
"His" house and pause in trance, an inner eye
Seeing the kids on stilts, up trees with books
(*Freddy the Magician*, Walter R. Brooks,
Another passionate synthesis), on wheels—
Red flash, blue flash; at each left shoulder sails
A small distortion of the cyclewind,
A shimmer; round the corner; gone—and stand
There *still* bereft. One dwarfish block away
"My" house, remodeled toy, the tree grown huge—
Distortions in the grain since Moving Day,
That sympathetic-magic-puppet stage.

Then Presto! flicked from memory's black sleeve
By sleight of (empty) hand, red, blue, a blur,
Thin silks of sense. The first quite as it were
External person, not a relative
Or family intimate, I ever knew
I loved—knew consciously and named the word—
Was Andy. Childish hero-worship blurred
By burgeoning hormones? No. It won't construe,
This Andy-love, as having been about

91

A boyfriend—though I'd "liked" boys, and was old
Enough to fill a training bra, and pulse
And burn like fury, stroking what poked out
Of Steve's or Charlie's bluejeans in the cold
November woods; but this meant something else.

Not having played Electra, though, it took
Me years of bafflement to get the two
Together, still imperfectly. I grew
Up irritated wild by any book—
E.g. *Farewell to Arms*—which understands
Love as a soup of sentiment and glands.

If that was true, my whole life made no sense.
—It's Moving Day, I'm carrying the baby,
A last walk round the block. I'm sad, he's crabby;
Glumly we pace the square circumference
Past Charlie's ... Andy's next, who yesterday
Put on a special puppet show by way

Of farewell gesture. They're in school, I hurt
All over, weirdly. —It's at least a year
Later, and no one else is anywhere
To watch the blotchy shape great sobs contort
Be wrestled by an angel to the floor:
Homesickness, shrieking from the sycamore.

In the sixth-grade class picture, taken that May,
I am the missing person. But Andy's there:
rolled cuffs, checkered shirt crossed and clasped
by a loose guardbelt, colorless cropped hair.
A quarter-century now I've mourned the boy
whose face—inscrutable slight scowl—that is.
Who suffered me, sometimes gladly. Whom I found

and lost as if by death, and so could neither
outgrow him and split loose, nor coax him round.

But—what if—what if somewhere lived a person
the boy grew up to be, yet the same boy?
Suppose he could be traced? that enough purpose
and cash would somewhere let me ring at a door
opened by the magician-puppeteer
at thirty-six or so in a three-piece suit—
some type of businessperson, perhaps a bank
vice-president? broker? on the small side, long plain
head like a lightbulb, balding . . . office quietly
plush, a varnished desk surmounted
by portraits: wife and two cute bulbheaded kids
in silver frames. "Do you remember me at all?"
I say, and Andy says, "Well, I'm *pretty* sure I do . . ."

Then why not simply latch the shutters of
The backward view? *Who cares* for history? Grieve
No more, tear up that picture, firmly love
Your loving friends; be sensible, believe
Tom Wolfe, not Proust. Instead—as primitive
Tribes would hail the onset of menses—five-
And-twenty summers late rejoice, and give
Thanks, for a latent magic come alive,
Just that!
　　　　Come casually as bedtime does.
You're kneeling in, one schoolnight, when for some
Reason, not yours, the switch whose time has come
Is thrown, the thought takes form and surfaces:
I *love* Andy
　　　　　　surprised, a bit nonplussed
By oddness, as of "gave birth to a ghost."

Who cares? I do. God help me, I do care
For all of that—how loving him connects
To chronic homelessness, but not to sex—
All of it. Find him, then. But how and where

To start on so, let's face it, meddlesome
A quest? One day he'll read this and find *me?*
Improbable. The only poetry
I ever heard him quote was something dumb—
        "Zingo, Stingo had a new trick:
        Kissed the wasps and made them sick . . ."—

From *Freddy the Magician.* Search the world,
Somewhere a short bald banker's doing tricks
To entertain his children, nine and six.
A wand sprouts flowers for Mom. Thin silks, unfurled

By flicks—red, blue, a blur—spurt from his fist.
The best trick is his rabbit-from-a-hat,
Both lent; the rabbit's name is Presto. That
Concludes our show. Two dazzled kids are kissed

And put to bed. Unnoticed, one blue silk
Uncrumples from a corner, something lifts
And rounds beneath it, cautiously it drifts
Along the baseboard, fading—blue of milk,

Translucent gauzy blue—sails toward the door,
Blue shimmer on the updraft, vanishing . . .
Could anyone shut out that sort of thing?
Last summer I went up the sycamore,

My reading tree, now mammoth. After all
Those years, I could have done it in my sleep
And never put a hand or foot wrong. Leap,
Walk up, leg over, catch a branch and haul

While pushing (instep), two-step to the top.
My same tree grown, myself its metaphor.
It's love that urges: Find where Andy is,

But, yes or no, this losing him must stop.
Let *me* stop then, till like my sycamore
I'm grounded in a place once partly his.

LIBRARY OF CONGRESS CATALOGING IN PUBLICATION DATA

Moffett, Judith, 1942-
Whinny moor crossing.

(Princeton series of contemporary poets)
I. Title.
PS3563.O29W45   1984   811'.54   83-43055
ISBN 0-691-06591-8
ISBN 0-691-01410-8 (pbk.)

Judith Moffett teaches in the English Department at the University
of Pennsylvania. Her other books include a volume of poetry
Keeping Time (Louisiana State University Press, 1976), and
James Merrill: An Introduction to the Poetry (Columbia Uni-
versity Press, 1984).